C.U.E.T. FINE ARTS EXAM GUIDE

DEVESH TANEJA

Copyright © Devesh Taneja
All Rights Reserved.

This book has been self-published with all reasonable efforts taken to make the material error-free by the author. No part of this book shall be used, reproduced in any manner whatsoever without written permission from the author, except in the case of brief quotations embodied in critical articles and reviews.

The Author of this book is solely responsible and liable for its content including but not limited to the views, representations, descriptions, statements, information, opinions and references ["Content"]. The Content of this book shall not constitute or be construed or deemed to reflect the opinion or expression of the Publisher or Editor. Neither the Publisher nor Editor endorse or approve the Content of this book or guarantee the reliability, accuracy or completeness of the Content published herein and do not make any representations or warranties of any kind, express or implied, including but not limited to the implied warranties of merchantability, fitness for a particular purpose. The Publisher and Editor shall not be liable whatsoever for any errors, omissions, whether such errors or omissions result from negligence, accident, or any other cause or claims for loss or damages of any kind, including without limitation, indirect or consequential loss or damage arising out of use, inability to use, or about the reliability, accuracy or sufficiency of the information contained in this book.

Made with ♥ on the Notion Press Platform
www.notionpress.com

For all those

Who dreamt to create art.

Contents

Contents

PREFACE

With immense pleasure and heartfelt gratitude, I present this compilation of questions, notes, and insights for aspiring artists and art enthusiasts. This book represents a labor of love, a testament to the transformative power of art, and a guiding companion for those embarking on the challenging yet rewarding journey of fine arts entrance examinations.

First and foremost, I express my deepest gratitude to my teachers, mentors, and guides who have been instrumental in shaping my understanding and appreciation of art. Their dedication, patience, and wisdom have not only honed my skills but also instilled in me the values of discipline, creativity, and perseverance. Their encouragement has been the cornerstone of my artistic endeavors, and it is their teachings that echo throughout the pages of this book.

Art, in its myriad forms, is a reflection of life—a medium through which we can express emotions, challenge norms, and connect with the world. This belief has been my compass, guiding me as I compiled this resource. I have drawn inspiration from the teachings of great artists, the philosophies of art history, and the practical experiences of my own journey as an art student. It is my hope that this book not only equips readers with the knowledge they need to excel in their entrance exams but also ignites their passion for art as a lifelong pursuit.

To my readers, I extend my heartfelt thanks for choosing this book as part of your preparatory journey. Whether you are a novice stepping into the world of art or someone seeking to deepen their understanding, this book is designed with you in mind. The questions, explanations, and notes aim to provide a holistic understanding of the topics most relevant to fine arts education in India. From the technical aspects of drawing and design to the nuanced histories of art movements, each section has been curated to challenge and inspire you.

As you turn these pages, remember that the journey to becoming an artist is as significant as the destination. The questions you answer, the notes you study, and the creative challenges you face will all contribute to your growth as an individual and as an artist. Let this book be a stepping stone on your path, a tool to unlock your potential, and a reminder that every great artist was once a beginner.

Finally, I would like to dedicate this effort to the boundless world of art and its ability to bring people together. May this book inspire you to dream bigger, work harder, and create more passionately. I am confident that with perseverance and dedication, each of you has the potential to make a meaningful impact in the world of art.

With my best regards and warm wishes for your future endeavors,

Devesh Taneja.

Notes

I

Art Fundamentals

The fundamentals of art are the essential building blocks that define visual art. These principles and elements are used by artists to create work that is aesthetically balanced, visually engaging, and conceptually meaningful. Understanding these fundamentals is crucial for anyone pursuing art or design, as it lays the groundwork for creative expression and the development of technical skills.

The core elements of art include:

Line: The most basic element, lines form the skeleton of any artwork. They can vary in thickness, length, and direction and can convey emotion or structure. A line can be straight or curved, horizontal, vertical, or diagonal, and can define the boundaries of shapes, forms, or create texture and pattern.

Shape: Shapes are created by lines or changes in color. They can be geometric (squares, circles, triangles) or organic (irregular shapes found in nature). Shapes are the basic units of design that help in constructing compositions.

Form: Form refers to the three-dimensional version of shape. It has depth, height, and width, and can be geometrical or organic, as seen in sculptures or architectural designs.

Color: One of the most powerful elements in art, color can evoke emotion, set the mood, or symbolize certain themes. Understanding the color wheel and how colors interact (complementary, analogous, etc.) is vital for creating a harmonious or contrasting composition.

Texture: Texture refers to the surface quality of an artwork, which can be real (tactile texture) or implied (visual texture). Artists often use different techniques to create texture, such as impasto in painting or the use of materials in sculpture.

Value: Value refers to the lightness or darkness of a color. It plays an essential role in creating contrast, depth, and mood within an artwork.

Space: Space refers to the area around, between, or within objects. It includes foreground, middle ground, and background and can be used effectively to create perspective and depth in a composition.

In addition to the elements of art, principles of design are equally important. These include:

Balance: The distribution of visual weight in an artwork. Balance can be symmetrical, asymmetrical, or radial.

Contrast: The juxtaposition of different elements (light vs. dark, smooth vs. rough) to create visual interest.

Emphasis: The focal point of a composition, achieved by drawing attention to a particular area through contrast, placement, or color.

Movement: The way a viewer's eye is guided through the artwork, often achieved through repetition, lines, or shapes.

Pattern: The repetition of elements in a predictable way, creating rhythm and harmony.

Unity: The sense that all elements in an artwork come together to form a cohesive whole.

Proportion and Scale: The relationship between the sizes of different elements within the artwork, contributing to its overall harmony or tension.

Mastery of these fundamentals is critical in all art forms, whether traditional or contemporary. By practicing these elements and principles, artists can develop their personal style and enhance their ability to communicate through visual media.

II

Indian Art and Artists

Indian art has a rich and diverse history that spans thousands of years, encompassing a variety of styles, techniques, and cultural influences. Indian art is known for its intricate details, vibrant colors, symbolic meanings, and deep connection to religion, culture, and history. The evolution of Indian art has been shaped by various dynasties, religions, and regional styles.

Ancient Indian Art: The earliest examples of Indian art date back to the Indus Valley Civilization, where we find sculptures, seals, and pottery that demonstrate an understanding of geometry and abstraction. One of the most notable early artworks is the Dancing Girl bronze sculpture, which showcases the naturalistic portrayal of the human form.

With the rise of Hinduism, Buddhism, and Jainism, religious themes began to dominate Indian art. The Ajanta Caves and Ellora Caves, with their stunning frescoes and sculptures, are prime examples of early Indian Buddhist art. The sculptures often depict scenes from the life of Buddha, and the intricate carvings on temple walls portray various deities and mythological stories.

Classical Indian Art: During the Gupta period (4th–6th centuries CE), Indian art reached a golden age. The Gupta period saw the development of highly refined sculptures and the production of exquisite cave paintings and temple architecture. The Bharhut and Sanchi Stupas are key examples of this period's remarkable achievements in sculpture.

Medieval and Mughal Art: The arrival of Islam in India brought a new set of artistic influences. Mughal art, which flourished between the 16th and 18th centuries, is known for its fusion of Persian, Central Asian, and Indian styles. Mughal miniature paintings, such as those created in the workshops of Emperor Akbar, depict court scenes, battles, and wildlife in rich detail. Artists like Raja Ravi Varma brought realism and a deep understanding of Western techniques to Indian art, producing iconic portraits of Hindu deities and historical figures.

Modern Indian Art: The 20th century witnessed a significant shift in Indian art, influenced by both Western modernism and the nationalistic movements within India. Artists like Amrita Sher-Gil, who studied in Europe, fused Western painting techniques with Indian themes, creating powerful portraits and self-portraits. M.F. Husain, often called the "Picasso of India," created vibrant, contemporary works that addressed social issues, while S.H. Raza and F.N. Souza explored abstraction and spirituality.

Other prominent Indian artists of the 20th century include Tyeb Mehta, Hema Upadhyay, Subodh Gupta, and Anish Kapoor, all of whom contributed to the modern and contemporary art scene, combining global influences with Indian cultural references.

Indian Art in the Contemporary Era: Today, Indian art is global in its reach. Artists like Bharti Kher, Atul Dodiya, Nalini Malani, and Jitish Kallat explore themes of identity, politics, history, and global interconnectedness in their works. Contemporary Indian art embraces various forms such as installation art, performance art, digital art, and video art, reflecting the dynamic socio-political landscape of India.

Indian art continues to evolve, blending traditional aesthetics with modern expression and pushing the boundaries of visual creativity.

III

Western Art History

Western art history traces the evolution of visual art from ancient civilizations through to modern times. This history reflects the cultural, social, and political changes in Europe and North America, with a rich diversity of movements, styles, and techniques that have shaped the course of art.

Ancient and Classical Art: Western art began with the art of the ancient Egyptians, Greeks, and Romans. Egyptian art is highly symbolic and adheres to strict conventions, with a focus on afterlife and divine rulers. In contrast, Greek and Roman art emphasized the human figure and realism. Greek artists such as Phidias created sculptural masterpieces like the Parthenon sculptures, while Roman art was renowned for its realistic portraiture and monumental architecture, including the Colosseum and the Pantheon.

Medieval Art: The fall of the Roman Empire in the 5th century CE marked the beginning of the medieval period, during which the Christian Church became the central patron of the arts. Byzantine art is known for its religious icons, gold mosaics, and stylized figures. The Gothic period (12th–16th centuries) produced soaring cathedrals with intricate stained glass windows and detailed sculptures, exemplified by artists like Giotto.

Renaissance Art: The Renaissance (14th–17th centuries) was a period of great cultural rebirth in Europe, marked by a renewed interest in classical antiquity. Artists like Leonardo da Vinci, Michelangelo, and Raphael revolutionized painting and sculpture with their mastery of human anatomy, perspective, and the use of light and shadow. The Last Supper and The Sistine Chapel ceiling are quintessential examples of Renaissance genius.

Baroque Art: The Baroque period (17th century) was characterized by dramatic expression, strong contrasts of light and dark (chiaroscuro), and a sense of movement. Artists such as Caravaggio, Peter Paul Rubens, and Rembrandt created emotionally charged works that conveyed religious and political themes. The Palace of Versailles in France is an iconic example of Baroque architecture.

Modern Art: The 19th and 20th centuries saw the birth of modernism, a movement that rejected traditional norms and embraced new forms of expression. Impressionism, led by Claude Monet and Pierre-Auguste Renoir, focused on capturing fleeting moments in light and color. Cubism, developed by Pablo Picasso and Georges Braque, fragmented objects into abstract forms, while Expressionism (e.g., Edvard Munch) sought to depict raw emotion. The rise of abstract art (e.g., Wassily Kandinsky) and surrealism (e.g., Salvador Dalí) further broke away from representational art, emphasizing the unconscious mind and the absurd.

Contemporary Art: In the 20th and 21st centuries, contemporary art embraced a variety of styles and mediums, including Pop Art, Conceptual Art, Minimalism, and Street Art. Artists like Andy Warhol, Roy Lichtenstein, and Damien Hirst challenged traditional concepts of art, using commercial imagery, mass production, and technology. The digital revolution has also had a profound impact on the art world, with artists exploring video art, interactive installations, and virtual reality as new modes of creative expression.

Western art history continues to evolve, with artists today responding to global issues, technological advancements, and cultural shifts. The diversity and innovation of Western art have made it a central part of the global art narrative.

IV
Contemporary Art

Contemporary art refers to the art created in the present day, typically by artists who are alive or working within the last few decades. It includes a vast array of styles, techniques, and mediums, and is often characterized by its diversity and global influence. Unlike traditional art movements that followed linear progressions, contemporary art embraces pluralism, where multiple trends and styles coexist.

Globalization and the Internet have played a significant role in shaping contemporary art. Artists today are exposed to a wide range of cultural influences, and they often tackle complex global issues such as politics, social justice, identity, environmental concerns, and technology.

In contemporary art, there is no single dominant style, but rather an emphasis on personal expression, conceptual thinking, and new media. Performance art, installation art, video art, digital art, and conceptual art are all part of the contemporary art world, each offering unique ways to interact with audiences.

Artists like Ai Weiwei, Banksy, and Jeff Koons have become internationally recognized for their ability to engage with social and political issues, often using unconventional methods and materials. Banksy, for example, is known for his street art that combines satire, humor, and social critique, while Jeff Koons creates large, shiny sculptures that explore consumerism and mass culture.

The boundaries between high art and popular culture have also become increasingly blurred in contemporary art, as seen in the rise of Pop Art in the 1960s, with artists like Andy Warhol and Roy Lichtenstein. Today, the influence of popular culture and media is ever-present, and many contemporary artists incorporate advertising, celebrity culture, and mass media into their work.

Art institutions, galleries, and art fairs have also played a significant role in shaping the visibility and commercialization of contemporary art. Events such as the Venice Biennale and the Art Basel fairs bring together artists, collectors, curators, and critics from around the world, highlighting the ongoing global dialogue in contemporary visual culture.

V

Art Movements and Styles

Art movements are often associated with particular periods, ideologies, and a collective group of artists whose work reflects a shared vision or style. Throughout history, art movements have played a pivotal role in defining artistic trends and pushing the boundaries of creative expression.

Renaissance (14th-17th centuries): A rebirth of classical ideals from ancient Greece and Rome. Artists like Leonardo da Vinci, Michelangelo, and Raphael emphasized perspective, naturalism, and the human form.

Baroque (17th century): Known for its dramatic use of light and shadow (chiaroscuro), emotional intensity, and ornate details. Artists such as Caravaggio, Peter Paul Rubens, and Rembrandt embraced movement, grandeur, and theatricality.

Impressionism (Late 19th century): A reaction against realism and the academic approach, focusing on capturing the fleeting effects of light and color. Claude Monet, Pierre-Auguste Renoir, and Edgar Degas painted en plein air, focusing on moments rather than details.

Cubism (Early 20th century): Developed by Pablo Picasso and Georges Braque, cubism fragmented objects into geometric shapes, offering multiple perspectives within a single composition. This movement was a pivotal departure from the single-point perspective of traditional art.

Surrealism (1920s-1950s): Focused on the unconscious mind, dreams, and irrational thought. Artists like Salvador Dalí, René Magritte, and Max Ernst explored surreal landscapes, dream-like figures, and symbolic imagery.

Abstract Expressionism (Mid-20th century): Characterized by spontaneous, emotional, and expressive brushstrokes, often without representational imagery. Artists like Jackson Pollock, Mark Rothko, and Willem de Kooning sought to express inner emotions through abstract forms.

Pop Art (1950s-1960s): A movement that drew inspiration from popular culture, mass media, and consumerism. Andy Warhol, Roy Lichtenstein, and Richard Hamilton blurred the boundaries between fine art and commercial products, with works often featuring icons of mass culture like celebrities, advertisements, and comic strips.

Minimalism (1960s-1970s): An abstract art movement that focused on simplicity, geometric forms, and the use of industrial materials. Artists like Donald Judd and Dan Flavin minimized the use of elements in their work, emphasizing the viewer's experience of the artwork.

Conceptual Art (1960s-present): Art where the idea or concept behind the work is more important than the finished object. Artists like Sol LeWitt and Joseph Kosuth focused on the intellectual process, often involving language, instructions, and audience participation.

Street Art (1980s-present): Often created in public spaces, street art includes graffiti, murals, and other forms of urban expression. Artists like Banksy and Shepard Fairey challenge social and political issues through provocative, visually striking works that are accessible to the masses.

VI
Famous Artists and Their Works

Throughout history, numerous artists have left an indelible mark on the art world, revolutionizing styles, techniques, and subject matter. Here are a few of the most influential figures:

Leonardo da Vinci (1452-1519): Known for masterpieces like The Mona Lisa and The Last Supper, Leonardo is one of the most famous Renaissance artists. His work explored human anatomy, perspective, and the natural world, blending art with science.

Michelangelo (1475-1564): A Renaissance sculptor, painter, and architect, Michelangelo created the iconic David and painted the ceiling of the Sistine Chapel, capturing human emotion and divine beauty in marble and fresco.

Pablo Picasso (1881-1973): A leader of the Cubist movement, Picasso's work evolved constantly, spanning many styles and periods. His famous works include Guernica, which is a reaction to the horrors of war, and Les Demoiselles d'Avignon, a groundbreaking piece in the development of modern art.

Frida Kahlo (1907-1954): Known for her deeply personal and symbolic self-portraits, Kahlo's work explored themes of identity, pain, and feminism. Her works, such as The Two Fridas and Self-Portrait with Thorn Necklace, are celebrated for their bold color and raw emotional intensity.

Andy Warhol (1928-1987): The leader of the Pop Art movement, Warhol transformed the way people thought about art and consumer culture. His famous works include Campbell's Soup Cans, Marilyn Diptych, and Gold Marilyn Monroe.

These artists, among others, have shaped the course of art history, influencing generations of artists and sparking ongoing debates about the nature of art, creativity, and cultural expression.

VII
Art Techniques and Materials

The techniques and materials used in art have evolved over time, reflecting changes in technology, culture, and artistic expression. From the use of natural pigments and brushes in prehistoric cave paintings to the adoption of synthetic materials in contemporary art, the choice of medium is integral to the creation and impact of an artwork.

Drawing Techniques: Drawing is the foundation of many art forms. Basic techniques include hatching (parallel lines), cross-hatching (intersecting lines), and stippling (dots). Drawing tools can range from pencils, charcoal, and pastels to ink and digital media. Artists use these to explore texture, form, and shading.

Painting Techniques: Various painting techniques have been developed over centuries, including:

Oil painting: Known for its rich texture and depth, oil painting allows for blending and layering, making it ideal for portraiture and landscapes.

Watercolor: Watercolors are transparent paints that flow and blend easily, making them popular for delicate and light effects.

Acrylic painting: Acrylics are fast-drying, versatile paints that can mimic both oil and watercolor effects, popular in modern and abstract art.

Fresco: A technique used in mural painting, where pigments are applied to wet plaster, allowing the artwork to become part of the wall surface.

Sculpture Techniques: Sculpture can be done in relief (carved into a flat surface), round (free-standing), or installation (site-specific). Traditional materials include stone, bronze, and clay, while modern sculptures use metal, wood, and even industrial materials.

Printmaking Techniques: Printmaking includes methods like etching, lithography, woodcut, and screen printing. Each technique has its unique approach to transferring an image onto paper, fabric, or other materials. Artists like Albrecht Dürer and Andy Warhol have used these techniques to mass-produce and distribute their work.

Digital Art: With the rise of technology, digital art has become a major field, encompassing digital painting, 3D modeling, animation, and interactive installations. Artists use software like Adobe Photoshop, Blender, and Procreate to create digital works that challenge traditional boundaries of art.

The materials artists choose influence the final appearance, texture, and message of their work, and modern technologies continue to provide new ways of creating and experiencing art.

VIII
Color Theory

Color theory is the study of how colors interact and how they can be used to create different effects and moods in art. It is a fundamental principle in visual arts, design, and art education. Color has the ability to influence emotion, depth, and harmony in a composition.

The Color Wheel: The color wheel is a circular diagram that represents colors in a spectrum. The primary colors—red, yellow, and blue—are the foundation. These can be mixed to create secondary colors—orange, green, and purple. Tertiary colors are created by mixing primary and secondary colors.

Color Harmony: Colors that are placed next to each other on the color wheel are called analogous colors, and they create harmony when used together. Complementary colors (colors opposite each other on the wheel, like red and green) create high contrast and can make each other appear more vibrant.

Warm and Cool Colors: Colors can be classified as warm (reds, oranges, yellows) or cool (blues, greens, purples). Warm colors tend to evoke feelings of energy, passion, and warmth, while cool colors are often associated with calm, tranquility, and coolness.

Value and Intensity: The value of a color refers to its lightness or darkness, which can be altered by adding white (tint) or black (shade). Intensity, or chroma, refers to the brightness or dullness of a color. A highly saturated color is considered intense, while a muted or desaturated color is less intense.

Psychological Effects of Color: Different colors evoke various emotional responses. For example, red is associated with energy, passion, and urgency, while blue conveys calmness, trust, and stability. Artists use these emotional associations strategically to communicate specific feelings or messages within their work.

Color Schemes: Artists and designers use various color schemes to achieve a certain effect. Common schemes include:

Monochromatic: Using variations of one color (light to dark) for a harmonious look.

Analogous: Combining colors next to each other on the color wheel, creating a unified, calming palette.

Complementary: Using colors that are opposite each other on the wheel for contrast and vibrancy.

Split-complementary: A variation of complementary colors, using one base color and two adjacent to its complementary.

Triadic: Using three evenly spaced colors on the color wheel to create a balanced and vibrant palette.

Color theory plays an important role not only in traditional painting but also in digital and graphic design, fashion, interior decorating, and advertising. Understanding how colors interact helps artists create depth, emphasize certain elements, and evoke emotional responses from viewers.

IX

Indian Art History

Indian art has a rich and diverse history that spans over several millennia. From the earliest rock art to contemporary practices, Indian art reflects the cultural, religious, and social changes that have occurred throughout the subcontinent.

Ancient Indian Art: The earliest traces of Indian art can be found in prehistoric cave paintings in regions like Bhimbetka in Madhya Pradesh. These paintings depict animals, human figures, and symbolic motifs. The Indus Valley Civilization (3300-1300 BCE) also produced finely crafted sculptures and seals, such as the famous dancing girl bronze sculpture, showcasing advanced artistic and technical skills.

Buddhist Art: As Buddhism spread throughout India in the 3rd century BCE, it had a profound influence on art. Early Buddhist art was centered around stupas and rock-cut cave temples like those at Ajanta and Ellora. The sculptures at these sites depicted the life of the Buddha, and the Madhya Pradesh and Sanchi sculptures represent key moments of his life. The use of Jataka tales (stories of the Buddha's past lives) was a prominent feature in Buddhist art.

Medieval Indian Art: During the Gupta period (4th-6th century CE), Indian art saw the development of classical traditions in sculpture and painting. The iconic sculptures of Gandhara and Mathura were created during this time, emphasizing idealized forms of human beauty and divine figures. The Chola dynasty (9th-13th century CE) produced some of the most exquisite temple sculptures in the world, with works like the Nataraja (Shiva as the Lord of Dance).

Mughal Art: The Mughal Empire (1526-1857) brought a fusion of Persian, Turkish, and Indian artistic traditions. Mughal rulers patronized monumental architecture, producing iconic buildings like the Taj Mahal. Mughal painting, known for its fine detail and vibrant colors, depicted courtly life, battles, and portraits of emperors. Artists such as Ustad Mansur and Bihzad became known for their miniature paintings, capturing both historical and natural scenes with exquisite detail.

Colonial and Modern Indian Art: During British colonial rule, Indian artists were influenced by Western techniques and styles. Raja Ravi Varma, a prominent figure in this era, combined traditional Indian themes with European academic realism. In the 19th and early 20th centuries, the Bengal School of Art, led by Abanindranath Tagore, sought to revive indigenous styles and push back against colonial dominance.

In the post-independence period, Indian art flourished with modernist movements. S. H. Raza, M. F. Husain, F. N. Souza, and Tyeb Mehta were among the pioneers who introduced modernism to India. These artists blended Western techniques with Indian traditions, reflecting the social, political, and cultural shifts of post-colonial India.

Contemporary Indian Art is marked by a mix of traditional and modern influences. Artists like Subodh Gupta, Bharti Kher, and Anish Kapoor have gained international recognition for their innovative and boundary-pushing works that address issues of identity, globalization, and modernity.

Indian art continues to evolve and reflects the nation's changing societal dynamics, spiritual beliefs, and diverse heritage.

X

Art in Society

Art plays a critical role in society, shaping cultural identities, influencing political movements, and reflecting social values. The relationship between art and society is dynamic; art can both mirror the world and challenge the status quo.

Historically, art has been used for religious, political, and social purposes. Ancient societies used art to convey spiritual beliefs, as seen in the temples of ancient Egypt, Greece, and India. Religious icons, such as the Egyptian statues of gods or the Christian iconography in medieval Europe, served as a means to connect with the divine.

Political art has been used as a tool for revolution, propaganda, and social commentary. In the 20th century, artists like Diego Rivera in Mexico and George Grosz in Germany used their art to critique social and political issues. In India, the art of Nandalal Bose and other artists associated with the Bengal School of Art reflected national pride and resistance to British colonial rule.

Art also plays a key role in social movements. Works of art have been powerful tools for advocating human rights, feminism, environmental awareness, and racial equality. For example, the Black Arts Movement in the U.S. or the Pictorialist photography movement in India, focused on the representation of marginalized communities.

In modern society, art continues to address pressing issues such as globalization, technology, identity, and the environment. The rise of digital art, street art, and public installations reflect how contemporary artists engage with new modes of communication and expression.

Art education and appreciation are crucial for the development of an informed, empathetic, and critical society. By engaging with art, individuals and communities can develop a deeper understanding of themselves, their culture, and the world around them.

XI
Indian Aesthetic Traditions

Indian aesthetic traditions refer to the deep philosophical and cultural understanding of beauty and art that has developed over thousands of years. These traditions are rooted in a variety of ancient texts, philosophies, and practices. Indian aesthetics is based on concepts that go beyond the visual appeal of art, incorporating sensory, emotional, and spiritual experiences.

Rasa Theory

The concept of rasa is central to Indian aesthetics. It refers to the emotional flavor or essence experienced by the audience when interacting with a work of art. The Natyashastra, a classical text on performing arts by the sage Bharata Muni, defines rasa as the emotional response that art should evoke. There are eight primary rasas: Shringara (love), Hasya (laughter), Karuna (compassion), Raudra (anger), Veera (bravery), Bhayanaka (fear), Bibhatsa (disgust), and Adbhuta (wonder).

These rasas are not only linked to performance art (like drama and dance) but also to visual art, music, and literature, creating a multidimensional aesthetic experience. Artists strive to communicate these emotions through their works, whether through facial expressions, body language, or the use of colors, textures, and composition in visual arts.

Sanskrit Poetics

Indian poetry, especially Sanskrit poetry, emphasizes a deep connection between language and emotions. The Sanskrit poetic tradition is rich with rules of meter (chandas) and rhyme, and its purpose was to stir emotional and intellectual responses in the reader or listener. The works of Kalidasa, Bharavi, and Bhavabhuti reflect this intricate relationship between form and content. The beauty in Sanskrit poetry lies not just in the words but also in their rhythm, musicality, and the layered meanings they convey.

Indian Temple Architecture

Indian architecture, particularly temple architecture, represents an essential aspect of Indian aesthetic traditions. It is deeply spiritual and symbolic, with every element of the temple – from the garbhagriha (sanctum sanctorum) to the shikhara (spire) – designed to represent cosmic order. The layout of temples follows strict principles defined by texts like the Vastu Shastra and Agama Shastra, which guide the placement of each architectural feature to create a harmonious space conducive to spiritual practice.

The intricacy of the sculptures on temple walls, especially in places like Khajuraho, Konark, and Hampi, reflect the traditional Indian view of art as a bridge between the material and the divine. The images of gods, goddesses, and celestial beings were crafted to evoke spiritual reverence and inspire meditation.

Indian Painting Traditions

Indian painting traditions are incredibly diverse, encompassing styles like Madhubani, Warli, Pattachitra, Tanjore, and Miniature paintings. These styles have evolved over centuries, often reflecting the local culture, religion, and social life.

For example, Madhubani painting from Bihar is known for its intricate patterns, vibrant colors, and themes related to nature, mythology, and folklore. Miniature paintings, such as those from Rajasthan and Mughal courts, are celebrated for their meticulous detail, rich color palettes, and fine brushwork, often depicting royal life, battles, or religious themes.

XII

Art Criticism and Analysis

Art criticism is the process of evaluating and interpreting works of art, assessing their aesthetic value, cultural significance, and emotional impact. Art criticism is a multifaceted practice that involves both subjective and objective analysis. Understanding art criticism requires familiarity with several core concepts:

Elements of Art

The elements of art are the fundamental building blocks used to create a work of art. These include:

Line: A mark made by a tool (pencil, brush, etc.) on a surface, which can vary in width, direction, and length. It can convey emotion and energy.

Shape: A two-dimensional area defined by boundaries or lines. Shapes can be geometric (squares, circles) or organic (irregular shapes like leaves or clouds).

Color: Color is one of the most important elements, and its use can create mood, contrast, and harmony. Artists often use color theory to achieve desired effects.

Texture: The surface quality of a work of art, which can be tactile or implied. Artists use texture to create depth and interest.

Space: The illusion of depth and perspective in two-dimensional works or the physical volume occupied by a sculpture or installation.

Form: In three-dimensional art, form refers to the volume and structure of the object, often achieved through the manipulation of light and shadow.

Principles of Design

While elements of art are the building blocks, principles of design guide how these elements are used to create a composition. Key principles include:

Balance: The distribution of visual weight in a composition, which can be symmetrical, asymmetrical, or radial.

Contrast: The use of opposing elements (light vs. dark, rough vs. smooth) to create interest and emphasize specific areas of the artwork.

Unity: The sense of wholeness or completeness in an artwork, where all elements work together harmoniously.

Emphasis: The creation of a focal point or area of interest in the composition, which draws the viewer's attention.

Movement: The suggestion of motion or the path the viewer's eye follows through the artwork.

Rhythm: A repetition of visual elements or patterns that creates a sense of movement or flow.

Contextual Analysis

Art criticism is not just about visual analysis but also about understanding the context in which the artwork was created. Contextual analysis involves examining the artist's intent, historical background, cultural influences, and societal impacts. For instance, understanding the political and social context of Guernica by Pablo Picasso adds layers to its interpretation as a response to the Spanish Civil War. The symbolic use of figures, such as the horse and the bull, communicates the chaos and suffering of war.

Interpretation and Judgment

Art criticism often concludes with an interpretation and a judgment of the work. Interpretation involves explaining the deeper meanings or messages the artwork conveys. This can involve exploring its symbolism, themes, or the emotional responses it evokes. Judgment, on the other hand, is an evaluation of the artwork's quality, success, and impact. Critics may argue about whether the work is innovative, aesthetically pleasing, or culturally significant.

Art History vs. Art Criticism

While art history looks at the evolution of art across time and examines the development of movements, periods, and artists, art criticism focuses on individual works of art and their analysis. Art historians deal with the context, provenance, and historical significance of art, whereas critics focus more on personal engagement, judgment, and emotional response to a work.

XIII

Cultural and Historical Context of Art

Art is often a reflection of the culture and time in which it was created. Understanding the cultural and historical context of an artwork is crucial for interpreting its meaning and significance. Throughout history, art has been used to comment on political, social, and religious issues, often in response to the changing circumstances of the time.

Art and Religion

Many of the world's great art traditions have been closely tied to religion. Christian art in medieval Europe, for instance, was created primarily to glorify God and teach religious stories to the illiterate population. Hindu and Buddhist art in India served similar purposes, with temples adorned with images of gods, goddesses, and scenes from religious texts.

Art and Politics

Throughout history, artists have used their work to make political statements. In 19th-century Europe, artists like Goya used their art to comment on social injustice and war. Communist art in Soviet Russia, such as Socialist Realism, used art to promote the state's ideology and glorify the working class. Art movements like Dada and Surrealism in the early 20th century were directly influenced by the political turmoil and aftermath of World War I.

Art and Society

Art has the power to reflect societal values, norms, and beliefs. For example, Victorian art often depicted idealized versions of domestic life and moral values, whereas Modernist art in the early 20th century sought to break away from these norms and embrace new ways of thinking. Feminist art movements in the 1970s and 1980s were a direct response to the marginalization of women in both art history and society.

Understanding the cultural and historical context of an artwork allows viewers to connect more deeply with its meaning, recognizing how it responds to or reflects the time and culture in which it was created.

XIV
Techniques and Mediums in Fine Art

The choice of medium and technique plays a vital role in defining the style and expression of an artwork. Artists use a wide range of materials and methods to bring their visions to life. Each medium offers unique properties that influence how art is created, perceived, and appreciated.

Painting Techniques and Mediums

Oil Painting: One of the most popular and versatile mediums in Western art, oil paint allows for rich color, smooth blending, and a wide range of textures. It is known for its slow drying time, which gives artists more time to work and adjust their compositions. Famous oil painters include Leonardo da Vinci, Rembrandt, and Vincent van Gogh.

Watercolor: Watercolor painting is characterized by its translucency, with pigments suspended in a water-based solution. Artists use watercolors to create delicate washes of color that can range from light and ethereal to vibrant and bold. Famous watercolorists include J.M.W. Turner and John Singer Sargent.

Acrylic: Acrylic paint dries faster than oil and can be used on a variety of surfaces, from canvas to wood. It offers both transparency and opacity, allowing for a range of effects from thin washes to thick impasto techniques. David Hockney and Mark Rothko were known for their innovative use of acrylics.

Fresco: This ancient technique involves painting on freshly applied plaster. The pigments bond with the wet plaster, making it a durable and long-lasting method of painting. Michelangelo's Sistine Chapel is a prime example of this technique, showcasing his mastery in the medium.

Drawing Techniques and Mediums

Pencil Drawing: Pencil is one of the most fundamental tools for sketching and drawing. It allows for a wide range of values and textures, from fine, delicate lines to dark, heavy shading. Artists like Albrecht Dürer used pencil drawings to explore intricate details and create studies for larger works.

Charcoal: Charcoal allows for rich, deep blacks and is ideal for dramatic contrasts and expressive line work. It is often used in portraiture and figure drawing, as seen in the works of Klimt and Rembrandt.

Ink: Ink can be used with pens or brushes to create detailed, precise lines. It can also be used in wash techniques to achieve softer effects. The famous Japanese ink drawings of Hokusai and Ukiyo-e artists highlight the use of ink in detailed illustrations.

Sculpture Techniques and Mediums

Stone Carving: The process of carving stone involves chiseling and sanding the material to shape it into the desired form. Stone sculptures often stand as monumental works, like the classical works of Michelangelo's David or the ancient Egyptian statues of pharaohs.

Bronze Casting: Bronze is a popular medium for sculptures because of its ability to be molded into intricate details and its durability. The lost-wax technique, used in bronze casting, allows for the creation of fine sculptures, such as the Greek statues of gods and Rodin's The Thinker.

Clay Sculpture: Artists have used clay for centuries to create expressive and tactile forms. The pottery of ancient civilizations is a testament to its long-standing role in art. Contemporary ceramic artists like Grayson Perry and Lucie Rie continue to push the boundaries of clay as an artistic medium.

Mixed Media and Installation Art

Mixed Media: Artists often combine a variety of materials—such as paint, paper, fabric, and found objects—into a single work. This approach can create complex textures and layers of meaning, as seen in the work of Robert Rauschenberg and Joseph Cornell.

Installation Art: Installation art involves creating large-scale works that transform the viewer's experience of space. Artists like Christo and Jeanne-Claude and Damien Hirst are known for their innovative use of space and materials in installations, challenging traditional ideas of what art is.

Digital Media

Digital Painting: With the advent of computers and software like Photoshop, artists can now create paintings directly on digital screens. This technique allows for endless possibilities with color, texture, and manipulation, with artists like David McLeod pushing the limits of digital art.

Video Art: Video as a medium for art has gained prominence in the 20th and 21st centuries, with artists like Bill Viola and Nam June Paik creating emotionally impactful works that explore time, motion, and human experience.

XV
Art Movements that Inspired ages

Art movements and styles are a significant aspect of art history. These movements reflect changes in society, culture, and technological advancements, as well as shifts in philosophical and artistic perspectives.

Renaissance

The Renaissance (14th-17th centuries) marked a profound shift in Western art, as it moved away from the medieval focus on religious themes and embraced humanism, naturalism, and classical antiquity. Artists like Leonardo da Vinci, Michelangelo, and Raphael produced works that celebrated the beauty of the human body, perspective, and proportion. The development of linear perspective revolutionized painting and gave a sense of depth and realism to artworks.

Baroque

The Baroque period (17th century) is characterized by dramatic lighting, intense emotion, and grandiose compositions. Artists like Caravaggio, Peter Paul Rubens, and Rembrandt used light and shadow (chiaroscuro) to create striking contrasts and bring a sense of movement to their paintings. Baroque art often conveyed powerful religious and royal themes, and its opulence mirrored the political and religious conflicts of the time.

Impressionism

In the late 19th century, the Impressionists broke from traditional painting styles by focusing on the effects of light, color, and everyday scenes. Rather than depicting subjects in fine detail, artists like Claude Monet, Edgar

Degas, and Pierre-Auguste Renoir captured fleeting moments, emphasizing atmosphere and emotion. The loose brushwork and bright color palettes of Impressionism broke away from the rigid academic standards of the time.

Cubism

Cubism, developed by Pablo Picasso and Georges Braque, challenged traditional perspectives by fragmenting objects into geometric shapes and presenting multiple viewpoints simultaneously. This revolutionary style, which emerged in the early 20th century, reflected the growing interest in abstraction and the complexity of modern life. Analytical Cubism focused on the deconstruction of objects, while Synthetic Cubism integrated collage and other materials into paintings.

Surrealism

The Surrealist movement (1920s-1930s) sought to express the unconscious mind and explore dreams, fantasies, and irrationality. Salvador Dalí, René Magritte, and Max Ernst created fantastical, often unsettling images that defied logical interpretation. Surrealism was influenced by the theories of Sigmund Freud and aimed to break away from the constraints of reality.

Abstract Expressionism

In the mid-20th century, Abstract Expressionism emerged as a movement focused on spontaneous, emotional expression and the exploration of non-representational forms. Artists like Jackson Pollock, Mark Rothko, and Willem de Kooning used abstraction as a means to convey deep psychological and emotional states. This style placed emphasis on the act of painting itself, often using large canvases and bold gestures.

Minimalism

Minimalism emerged in the late 1950s as a response against the emotional intensity of Abstract Expressionism. Donald Judd, Dan Flavin, and Frank Stella created artworks characterized by simple, geometric forms and industrial materials. Minimalist art sought to strip away any narrative or emotional content, focusing on the pure form and the materials used.

Pop Art

Pop Art emerged in the 1950s as an exploration of consumer culture, mass media, and popular imagery. Artists like Andy Warhol, Roy Lichtenstein, and Richard Hamilton appropriated images from advertising, comics, and celebrity culture, transforming them into high art. The movement was both a celebration and a critique of consumerism, drawing attention to the commercialization of culture.

XVI
Art as a Social Commentary

Throughout history, art has served as a means of reflecting and challenging societal norms. It can question authority, expose injustice, and highlight societal issues. Artists have often used their work to comment on politics, human rights, environmental concerns, and the human condition.

Political Art

Political art addresses power structures, oppression, and the struggle for justice. Diego Rivera, for example, used his murals to convey messages about class struggles and the rights of workers in Mexico. Similarly, Goya's The Third of May 1808 dramatically illustrates the horrors of war and the brutality of French occupation in Spain.

In India, political art became a form of resistance during the independence movement. Artists like Abanindranath Tagore used art to portray the cultural revival and nationalism of the time. Modern political artists, such as Raja Ravi Varma, used mythological subjects to subtly comment on social issues, like the subjugation of women.

Environmental Art

As global environmental concerns have grown, artists have increasingly engaged with ecological issues through their works. The Earth Art movement of the 1960s and 1970s involved creating large-scale works that interacted directly with nature, such as Robert Smithson's Spiral Jetty. Contemporary environmental art also raises awareness of issues like deforestation, pollution, and climate change. For instance, Andy

Goldsworthy creates ephemeral sculptures using natural materials, highlighting the fleeting nature of beauty and the need to preserve the environment.

Social Issues and Human Rights

Art has been an essential tool for advocating human rights, representing marginalized voices, and confronting social issues such as race, gender inequality, and poverty. Photographers like Dorothea Lange and James Nachtwey have documented social injustice and human suffering through their lens. Meanwhile, contemporary performance artists like Tania Bruguera use their bodies to engage directly with issues of migration, censorship, and political repression.

XVII
Art Education and Career Paths

Art education is the foundation upon which artists build their skills, knowledge, and career. Fine arts colleges and universities offer a variety of programs to nurture artistic talent and creativity, ranging from undergraduate to postgraduate levels.

Types of Art Degrees

Bachelor of Fine Arts (BFA): This undergraduate program allows students to explore different art forms while developing technical skills and creativity. The curriculum typically includes courses in drawing, painting, sculpture, printmaking, digital media, and art history.

Master of Fine Arts (MFA): This is a postgraduate program that allows students to specialize in a particular medium or genre of art. An MFA provides students with the opportunity to refine their artistic voice, engage in critical analysis, and produce a body of work for public display or exhibition.

Diploma Courses in Fine Arts: Many institutes offer diploma courses that focus on specific areas like graphic design, photography, animation, or textile design. These programs are shorter and more focused than degree programs, providing students with specialized skills for particular careers.

Art as a Career

Art offers a wide range of career opportunities, not just as an artist but in other sectors that require artistic expertise. Graphic design, illustration, and advertising are all industries that require the skills of trained artists.

Additionally, art history, museum curation, and gallery management provide pathways for those interested in the academic and curatorial side of the art world.

Conclusion

Art education prepares students to embark on a career as artists or in related fields such as art history, design, and curation. It provides not only technical skills but also critical thinking and the ability to engage with the world through creativity. Whether an artist or an art professional, the pursuit of art involves continuous learning and adaptation to new techniques, theories, and cultural contexts.

XVIII
Psychology of Art

The psychology of art delves into how human cognition, perception, and emotions influence the creation and reception of art. It examines how the brain processes visual stimuli and how art affects our psychological state. The psychological impact of art is an area of study that bridges art theory, cognitive psychology, and neuroscience. It also explores how different forms of art—visual art, music, dance, and performance—evoke emotions, memories, and thoughts in the audience.

Perception and Interpretation of Art

Psychologists have studied how people perceive art, suggesting that certain principles guide visual perception. Gestalt theory, for example, emphasizes how we tend to group elements in an artwork into unified wholes. Proximity, similarity, and continuity are Gestalt principles that help the brain make sense of complex compositions. Color psychology is another area of interest. Warm colors like red and yellow evoke energy and excitement, while cool colors such as blue and green tend to calm the viewer. These principles are applied by artists consciously or subconsciously to create specific effects.

Perception is also influenced by the viewer's cultural background and personal experiences. For example, the way a person from an agricultural society might interpret a landscape painting might differ from someone in an urban environment. Framing is another factor in how art is interpreted—how the artist positions the subject within the frame, the relationship between foreground and background, and the inclusion or exclusion of certain elements can dramatically alter the message of the artwork.

Art and Emotion

The relationship between art and emotion has been central to both the creation and consumption of art. The ability of art to evoke emotional responses is perhaps one of the most powerful aspects of art. Art can produce aesthetic emotions, such as awe, wonder, or joy, as well as more intense feelings like sorrow, anger, or anxiety. These emotional reactions can arise from both representational content—such as tragic subject matter—and formal qualities, such as the dynamic use of line, shape, color, and composition.

Artists often use these emotional responses to communicate themes of human experience. For instance, Edvard Munch's The Scream conveys existential angst, while Frida Kahlo's self-portraits express themes of pain, identity, and resilience. The viewer's emotional connection to an artwork can be deeply personal, influenced by their own life experiences.

Art Therapy

Art therapy is a psychological treatment that uses creative expression to help individuals explore their emotions, improve mental health, and solve problems. By engaging in art-making, patients are often able to express feelings they might not be able to articulate with words. Art therapy can be particularly helpful for individuals dealing with trauma, depression, or anxiety, and it has been used in a variety of therapeutic settings, including hospitals, schools, and rehabilitation centers.

Art therapists often guide individuals to create art that reflects their emotions and thought processes, encouraging self-reflection and insight. The process of creating art, whether abstract or representational, becomes a method for patients to communicate and process complex emotions, as well as a way to build self-confidence and cope with challenging situations.

XIX

Visual Culture

Visual culture is the study of how visual images and symbols are used and interpreted within a society. This broad area of study covers everything from fine art to mass media, advertising, fashion, and digital media. Visual culture explores the role that visual images play in shaping our perception of the world and how we communicate ideas through imagery.

The Role of Mass Media in Visual Culture

The rise of mass media, including television, film, and the internet, has significantly impacted visual culture. These mediums provide a platform for artists, advertisers, filmmakers, and influencers to shape public opinion and create trends. The study of visual culture involves understanding how mass media employs images to communicate messages about identity, politics, and consumerism.

For example, the advertising industry uses visually persuasive techniques, such as compelling imagery and strategic use of color, to influence consumer behavior. The fashion industry relies on visual culture to create styles that convey wealth, status, or rebellion, depending on the cultural context. In the age of social media, platforms like Instagram have become a space where individuals shape their public personas through carefully curated images.

Digital Visual Culture

With the rapid development of digital technology, visual culture has entered a new era. Digital art, virtual reality (VR), and augmented reality (AR) have become new modes of artistic expression and interaction. Artists are using digital platforms to create immersive environments and experiences that blur the lines between reality and the digital world. For instance, digital installations or 3D art allow viewers to experience art in new and dynamic ways, challenging traditional notions of space and form.

Moreover, the proliferation of memes and GIFs in the digital realm demonstrates how new forms of visual communication are constantly evolving. These digital expressions often convey humor, political messages, or social commentary in an easily shareable format, influencing online cultures and collective memory.

Globalization and Visual Culture

Globalization has also played a significant role in the development of visual culture. With the advent of the internet and social media, images from different parts of the world are now easily accessible to everyone. This interconnectedness has led to the spread of cultural symbols and visual trends, while also giving rise to new hybrid forms of visual culture. Global visual culture increasingly reflects the blending of different cultural traditions and influences, as well as the influence of global issues like climate change, migration, and digital technology.

Art, fashion, and visual media are now consumed across national borders, leading to the rise of global icons like K-pop, Hollywood, and global brands. This interconnectedness has raised questions about cultural appropriation, authenticity, and the ethical implications of globalized visual culture.

XX
Art and Politics

Art and politics have long been intertwined. Artists have often used their work to respond to political events, challenge authority, and comment on social justice issues. Political art can serve as a tool for resistance, protest, or propaganda, depending on the artist's intent.

Art as Protest

Art has historically been used as a form of protest against political regimes, social injustices, and wars. The Dada movement, for example, arose as a response to the horrors of World War I, rejecting traditional values and embracing chaos and absurdity as a critique of the societal systems that led to war. Similarly, Guernica by Pablo Picasso was created in response to the bombing of the Spanish town of Guernica by Nazi forces, symbolizing the devastation caused by war.

In India, artists like S.H. Raza and M.F. Husain have used their art to critique political events and comment on national identity, independence, and unity. Contemporary political artists engage with issues such as climate change, migration, and gender rights, often using street art, installation art, and performance art as methods of political expression.

Art as Propaganda

While art can serve as a vehicle for protest, it can also be used by governments and political groups as a form of propaganda. Totalitarian regimes, such as those in Nazi Germany or Soviet Russia, used art to promote political ideologies and suppress dissent. State-sponsored art was often highly idealized and depicted the leader as a heroic figure or the nation as invincible.

XXI

Art and the Environment

The intersection of art and the environment is a growing field that examines how artists respond to environmental issues, such as climate change, pollution, and the degradation of natural landscapes. Art has the potential to raise awareness of these issues, engage the public in environmental activism, and offer new ways of thinking about the natural world.

Environmental Art

Environmental art, also known as land art or earth art, emerged in the 1960s and 1970s as a response to the growing environmental concerns of the time. Artists like Robert Smithson and Andy Goldsworthy used the natural environment itself as both their medium and subject matter. Smithson's Spiral Jetty, a large earthwork constructed in the Great Salt Lake of Utah, is one of the most iconic examples of land art. This work interacts with the landscape and changes over time, as the forces of nature alter the site.

Goldsworthy's work, which often involves creating sculptures from natural materials such as stones, leaves, and ice, emphasizes the impermanence of the natural world. By working with the materials of the earth, these artists seek to foster a deeper understanding of our relationship with the environment and the transient nature of the landscape.

Eco-Art and Activism

In recent years, art has increasingly been used as a form of environmental activism. Eco-artists focus on environmental issues such as climate change, deforestation, pollution, and species extinction. These artists aim to raise awareness, inspire action, and promote sustainability. Artists like Mel Chin and Christo and Jeanne-Claude have worked on large-scale environmental projects that draw attention to environmental degradation and encourage viewers to think critically about the impact of human activity on the planet.

Eco-art can take many forms, including installations, performance art, and community projects. Some artists engage in upcycling, creating art from recycled or repurposed materials to highlight the importance of reducing waste. Others may create interactive pieces that allow viewers to participate in environmental actions or directly engage with environmental concerns.

Through art, environmental messages can be communicated in a visceral and emotional way, motivating individuals and communities to take steps toward a more sustainable future. Art has the power to not only reflect the state of the environment but also to inspire change by encouraging new ways of thinking and acting.

XXII

Photography and its Evolution in Art

Photography, from its inception in the early 19th century, has evolved significantly, from a technical invention to an art form with its own history, movements, and techniques. It has played a crucial role in shaping how we see the world, documenting history, and influencing artistic trends.

The Birth of Photography

Photography was invented in the 1830s, with early pioneers like Joseph Nicéphore Niépce and Louis Daguerre developing the first photographic processes. Daguerre's daguerreotype, introduced in 1839, was the first widely used method for producing photographs, and it marked the beginning of photography's journey as a means of capturing reality. The invention of photography gave artists a new tool to document life, and the technique quickly became popular for portraits and landscape photography.

While photography initially focused on realism and technical precision, it was soon embraced by artists for its ability to capture moments in time, offering a new perspective on the world. Photography allowed artists to explore the boundaries of representation, challenging the traditions of painting and drawing.

The Transition to Fine Art

By the late 19th century, photography had transitioned from being purely documentary or utilitarian to an acknowledged form of art. Early pioneers such as Alfred Stieglitz, Edward Weston, and Ansel Adams explored the expressive potential of the medium, capturing landscapes, portraits, and still life in ways that were more artistic than realistic. The establishment of organizations like the Photo-Secession in 1902, led by Stieglitz, was instrumental in promoting photography as a fine art.

The role of the photographer as an artist became widely recognized during the Pictorialist movement, which sought to emphasize mood and atmosphere in photographs. Pictorialists manipulated images through soft focus and darkroom techniques, drawing on the aesthetics of painting and drawing. This shift allowed photographers to gain recognition not just as documenters but as creators of visual art.

The Rise of Modernist Photography

As the 20th century progressed, the development of modernist movements had a profound impact on photography. Modernism, with its emphasis on abstraction, form, and experimentation, influenced many photographers to experiment with new techniques and subject matter. Man Ray and Laszlo Moholy-Nagy were key figures in the development of avant-garde photography, using techniques like photograms and light manipulation to challenge the traditional boundaries of photography.

Photographers also began to embrace more experimental approaches to the medium, such as surrealism, where images were manipulated or combined to create dream-like, irrational juxtapositions. The use of photography for social critique and commentary became more pronounced during this period. Photographers like Dorothea Lange and Walker Evans used photography as a means of documenting social issues, particularly the effects of the Great Depression, with their powerful, humanistic images of poverty and struggle.

Contemporary Photography

In the contemporary era, photography has expanded beyond traditional methods, with digital photography, digital manipulation, and new technologies allowing for unprecedented creativity. The invention of the digital camera in the late 20th century revolutionized the medium, enabling photographers to experiment with techniques that were once impossible.

The use of Photoshop and other digital editing tools has introduced new possibilities for creative expression, making it easier for photographers to manipulate and enhance images. This has led to the rise of conceptual photography, where the idea behind the photograph often becomes more important than the image itself. Cindy Sherman and Jeff Wall are known for their conceptual works, which often explore identity, gender, and the nature of representation.

Photography has become a key medium in contemporary art, often seen as an interdisciplinary tool that crosses into other visual arts like painting, sculpture, and digital art. It is used to explore themes ranging from memory and identity to social issues and technological advancements.

XXIII
Art Criticism: Methods and Approaches

Art criticism is a field that examines, analyzes, and evaluates works of art. It involves various approaches and methodologies, each offering a different lens through which to view and interpret art.

Formalism

Formalism is an approach to art criticism that focuses on the visual elements of the artwork, such as composition, color, line, texture, and form. This approach emphasizes how these elements interact within the artwork rather than focusing on the subject matter or the artist's intentions. Formalists believe that the aesthetic value of art lies in its formal qualities, and they evaluate works based on their visual harmony and unity.

A key figure in formalism is Clement Greenberg, who argued that the best art is art that emphasizes its medium. For example, Greenberg praised Abstract Expressionism because it focused on the physical act of painting and the inherent qualities of paint, such as texture and color.

Iconography

Iconography is an approach to art criticism that focuses on the symbolic content of the artwork. It involves analyzing the symbols, imagery, and themes within the work to uncover deeper meanings and connections to cultural, religious, or historical contexts. Iconographers often examine the use of symbols and metaphors in religious or mythological art, for example, in order to understand the cultural and social messages conveyed.

Art historians like Erwin Panofsky contributed significantly to the field of iconography, developing methods for interpreting visual symbols and uncovering hidden meanings in artworks. In his work, Panofsky focused on identifying symbols and their significance within specific historical and cultural contexts.

Contextualism

Contextualism is an approach that emphasizes the historical, cultural, and social context in which the artwork was created. This method considers the artist's life, the period in which the work was made, and the societal influences that shaped the artwork. Contextualists argue that understanding the context surrounding an artwork is essential for fully appreciating its meaning and significance.

This approach is widely used in art history, where critics and scholars examine the cultural, political, and historical backdrop of an artwork to understand its message. For example, Guernica is often interpreted in the context of the Spanish Civil War, with critics focusing on how Picasso's work reflects the horrors of war and the suffering of the Spanish people during that time.

Feminist Criticism

Feminist art criticism examines the representation of gender in art, focusing on the ways in which women are portrayed and how gender dynamics influence artistic production and reception. Feminist critics like Linda Nochlin and Griselda Pollock have challenged the traditional male-dominated narrative of art history and examined the role of women artists in shaping the art world.

Feminist art criticism also highlights how artworks often perpetuate gender stereotypes and societal expectations. In recent years, feminist art critics have analyzed how contemporary artists use their work to critique patriarchy, explore female identity, and empower women.

Postcolonial Criticism

Postcolonial art criticism examines how colonialism and its aftermath have shaped artistic practices and representations. It focuses on how art reflects issues of race, identity, and power, especially in postcolonial societies. Postcolonial critics argue that art is a tool of colonial discourse and can either reinforce or resist colonial ideologies.

Artists from former colonies have used their work to reclaim their cultural heritage and challenge the legacies of colonialism. The work of artists like Yinka Shonibare and The Guerrilla Girls addresses issues of race, cultural appropriation, and the politics of representation in contemporary art.

Multiple Choice Question

Part 1: General Knowledge of Fine Arts

Who painted the Mona Lisa?

A. Vincent van Gogh

B. Leonardo da Vinci

C. Michelangelo

D. Pablo Picasso

Answer: B

Ajanta Caves are famous for their:

A. Sculptures

B. Frescoes

C. Rock carvings

D. Calligraphy

Answer: B

Which color is formed by mixing red and blue?

A. Purple

B. Orange

C. Green

D. Brown

Answer: A

The famous painting "Starry Night" was created by:

A. Claude Monet

B. Vincent van Gogh

C. Salvador Dalí

D. Rembrandt

Answer: B

Which medium is commonly used in watercolor painting?

A. Canvas

B. Paper

C. Wood

D. Metal

Answer: B

In the principles of design, balance refers to:

A. Symmetry and asymmetry

B. Color distribution

C. Text alignment

D. Shape contrast

Answer: A

Which Indian artist is known as the "Father of Modern Indian Art"?

A. Amrita Sher-Gil

B. Raja Ravi Varma

C. Jamini Roy

D. Abanindranath Tagore

Answer: B

What is the primary binder in oil paints?

A. Water

B. Turpentine

C. Linseed oil

D. Gum Arabic

Answer: C

The term "Fresco" refers to:

A. Painting on dry plaster

B. Painting on wet plaster

C. Oil painting

D. Charcoal sketching

Answer: B

The Taj Mahal is an example of which architectural style?

A. Gothic

B. Mughal

C. Victorian

D. Dravidian

Answer: B

Part 2: Techniques and Tools

Which tool is used for sculpting?

A. Chisel

B. Easel

C. Palette

D. Charcoal

Answer: A

What is "perspective" in drawing?

A. Mixing colors

B. Creating depth and dimension

C. Drawing geometric shapes

D. Outlining a figure

Answer: B

What is the term for the lightness or darkness of a color?

A. Hue

B. Value

C. Saturation

D. Tone

Answer: B

Which surface is most suitable for oil painting?

A. Canvas

B. Plastic

C. Glass

D. Paper

Answer: A

Which brush type is best for creating fine details?

A. Flat brush

B. Round brush

C. Fan brush

D. Filbert brush

Answer: B

What is the name of the technique where light and dark tones are used to create the illusion of depth?

A. Chiaroscuro

B. Impasto

C. Pointillism

D. Hatching

Answer: A

Which term describes the quality of a surface in art?

A. Texture

B. Pattern

C. Form

D. Shape

Answer: A

What is the primary pigment source for natural dyes?

A. Metal oxides

B. Organic materials

C. Synthetic chemicals

D. Glass particles

Answer: B

In ceramics, the process of heating clay to make it hard is called:

A. Molding

B. Firing

C. Casting

D. Glazing

Answer: B

Which tool is used for smoothing surfaces in sculpture?

A. Sandpaper

B. Chisel

C. File

D. Mallet

Answer: A

Part 3: Indian Art and Culture

Who painted "Shakuntala"?

A. Nandalal Bose

B. Raja Ravi Varma

C. Rabindranath Tagore

D. S.H. Raza

Answer: B

Which dance form originated in Kerala?

A. Kathak

B. Kathakali

C. Odissi

D. Manipuri

Answer: B

Madhubani painting originated in which state of India?

A. Rajasthan

B. Bihar

C. Gujarat

D. Maharashtra

Answer: B

The Kailasa temple is located in which cave complex?

A. Ajanta

B. Ellora

C. Elephanta

D. Badami

Answer: B

The theme of most miniature paintings from Mughal art revolves around:

A. War scenes

B. Court life

C. Nature

D. Folk tales

Answer: B

Part 4: Art History and Movements

Cubism was pioneered by which artists?

A. Picasso and Braque

B. Van Gogh and Gauguin

C. Monet and Renoir

D. Matisse and Derain

Answer: A

Which art movement emphasized speed and technology in the early 20th century?

A. Futurism

B. Impressionism

C. Surrealism

D. Expressionism

Answer: A

The Bauhaus School was established in which country?

A. France

B. Germany

C. Italy

D. USA

Answer: B

Pointillism is a technique most associated with which artist?

A. Georges Seurat

B. Claude Monet

C. Henri Matisse

D. Wassily Kandinsky
Answer: A
    Which art movement is Salvador Dalí associated with?
A. Impressionism
B. Cubism
C. Surrealism
D. Fauvism
Answer: C
    Which period of Indian art is known for its Buddhist stupas?
A. Gupta period
B. Mauryan period
C. Mughal period
D. Chola period
Answer: B
    The famous "Vitruvian Man" drawing was created by:
A. Raphael
B. Leonardo da Vinci
C. Donatello
D. Michelangelo
Answer: B
    The term "Impressionism" originated from a painting by:
A. Edgar Degas
B. Claude Monet
C. Paul Cézanne
D. Pierre-Auguste Renoir
Answer: B
    What is the main characteristic of abstract art?
A. Depicting realistic subjects
B. Using geometrical patterns
C. Non-representational forms
D. Detailed storytelling
Answer: C
    The Gandhara School of Art is known for its:
A. Hindu temples
B. Buddhist sculptures
C. Mughal paintings
D. Jain manuscripts
Answer: B

Part 5: Indian Folk and Tribal Art

Warli painting originates from which Indian state?

A. Maharashtra

B. Madhya Pradesh

C. Gujarat

D. Rajasthan

Answer: A

Pattachitra is a traditional art form of which state?

A. Odisha

B. West Bengal

C. Bihar

D. Assam

Answer: A

Phad painting is primarily associated with which state?

A. Gujarat

B. Rajasthan

C. Punjab

D. Uttar Pradesh

Answer: B

Which of the following is NOT a tribal art form?

A. Gond

B. Pichwai

C. Madhubani

D. Kalamkari

Answer: D

Kalamkari painting is traditionally done on:

A. Canvas

B. Silk

C. Wood

D. Cotton fabric

Answer: D

Part 6: Design Principles and Aesthetics

Which principle of design relates to the visual weight of elements?

A. Contrast

B. Balance

C. Rhythm

D. Unity

Answer: B

Repetition in design creates a sense of:
A. Harmony
B. Chaos
C. Contrast
D. Perspective
Answer: A

The golden ratio is often used in art to achieve:
A. Symmetry
B. Proportion
C. Asymmetry
D. Texture
Answer: B

Complementary colors are located where on the color wheel?
A. Next to each other
B. Opposite each other
C. Forming a triangle
D. In a square arrangement
Answer: B

In design, the space around objects is referred to as:
A. Texture
B. White space
C. Alignment
D. Pattern
Answer: B

What does "emphasis" in design refer to?
A. Visual focus or attention on a particular area
B. The repetitive use of an element
C. Maintaining proportion in composition
D. Arranging elements symmetrically
Answer: A

Which type of balance is used when elements radiate from a central point?
A. Symmetrical
B. Asymmetrical
C. Radial
D. Horizontal
Answer: C

Unity in design refers to:

A. Contrasting elements

B. A harmonious arrangement

C. Repeated patterns

D. High visual tension

Answer: B

What is a monochromatic color scheme?

A. Using only one color and its shades

B. Combining opposite colors

C. Using three adjacent colors

D. Mixing warm and cool colors

Answer: A

Typography in design focuses on:

A. Color schemes

B. Text arrangement and fonts

C. Image placement

D. Proportions in layout

Answer: B

Part 7: Art Techniques and Media

Which medium uses wax-based pigments?

A. Acrylic

B. Tempera

C. Oil

D. Encaustic

Answer: D

A palette knife is used for:

A. Mixing paints or applying thick layers

B. Drawing outlines

C. Etching designs

D. Cutting paper

Answer: A

The process of printing from a metal plate with incised lines is called:

A. Etching

B. Relief printing

C. Silk screen printing

D. Monoprinting

Answer: A

Acrylic paint can be thinned with:
A. Water
B. Turpentine
C. Linseed oil
D. Varnish
Answer: A

Charcoal is commonly used for:
A. Color washes
B. Fine detailing
C. Sketching and shading
D. Layering paints
Answer: C

Which of the following is a dry medium?
A. Watercolor
B. Oil pastels
C. Acrylic
D. Tempera
Answer: B

The process of applying multiple layers of thin paint is known as:
A. Glazing
B. Impasto
C. Scumbling
D. Stippling
Answer: A

Which tool is NOT typically used in printmaking?
A. Roller
B. Chisel
C. Brayer
D. Squeegee
Answer: B

Gouache is most similar to which other medium?
A. Oil paint
B. Watercolor
C. Acrylic
D. Charcoal
Answer: B

In photography, the term "aperture" refers to:
A. Shutter speed

B. Lens opening
C. Light sensitivity
D. Focal length
Answer: B

What is the technique of painting with dots of color called?
A. Pointillism
B. Stippling
C. Glazing
D. Hatching
Answer: A

Which art medium is commonly used for quick sketches?
A. Ink
B. Charcoal
C. Oil paints
D. Encaustic
Answer: B

The technique of blending colors smoothly in painting is called:
A. Layering
B. Feathering
C. Sfumato
D. Burnishing
Answer: C

In ceramics, the process of applying a glass-like coating is called:
A. Firing
B. Glazing
C. Molding
D. Casting
Answer: B

Which type of paint dries the fastest?
A. Acrylic
B. Oil
C. Watercolor
D. Gouache
Answer: A

Part 8: General Art Knowledge

Which term describes the arrangement of objects in a painting?
A. Perspective
B. Composition

C. Linework

D. Palette

Answer: B

What is a common purpose of using a grid in drawing?

A. Adding texture

B. Achieving proportion and alignment

C. Creating perspective

D. Shading objects

Answer: B

A mural is:

A. A painting done on paper

B. A sculpture made from clay

C. A large-scale painting on a wall

D. A drawing with chalk

Answer: C

The term "contrapposto" is used in reference to:

A. Sculpture pose with weight on one leg

B. A type of mosaic

C. A painting method

D. Perspective drawing

Answer: A

Which Indian temple is famous for its erotic sculptures?

A. Konark Sun Temple

B. Khajuraho Temples

C. Brihadeeswarar Temple

D. Meenakshi Temple

Answer: B

What does the term "impasto" refer to?

A. Transparent layers of paint

B. Thick application of paint

C. A specific type of brushstroke

D. Soft blending of colors

Answer: B

Which type of art involves creating patterns by cutting paper?

A. Origami

B. Papercut art

C. Collage

D. Calligraphy

Answer: B

Which artist is famous for the series "Campbell's Soup Cans"?

A. Andy Warhol

B. Jackson Pollock

C. Roy Lichtenstein

D. Mark Rothko

Answer: A

What does the term "hue" refer to in art?

A. The brightness of a color

B. The name of a color

C. The saturation of a color

D. The lightness or darkness of a color

Answer: B

The famous painting "The Persistence of Memory" was created by:

A. Salvador Dalí

B. René Magritte

C. Pablo Picasso

D. Edvard Munch

Answer: A

Part 9: Famous Artists and Their Works

Who is the artist behind "Guernica"?

A. Pablo Picasso

B. Henri Matisse

C. Claude Monet

D. Edvard Munch

Answer: A

Michelangelo painted the Sistine Chapel ceiling in which location?

A. Rome

B. Vatican City

C. Florence

D. Milan

Answer: B

"The Scream" is a famous work by:

A. Edvard Munch

B. Gustav Klimt

C. Salvador Dalí

D. Paul Gauguin

Answer: A

Who is known for painting "The Last Supper"?
A. Raphael
B. Michelangelo
C. Leonardo da Vinci
D. Titian
Answer: C

Which artist is associated with the painting "Girl with a Pearl Earring"?
A. Johannes Vermeer
B. Rembrandt
C. Pieter Bruegel
D. Jan van Eyck
Answer: A

"Sunflowers" is a series by which artist?
A. Claude Monet
B. Vincent van Gogh
C. Paul Cézanne
D. Henri Rousseau
Answer: B

The painting "The Birth of Venus" was created by:
A. Sandro Botticelli
B. Caravaggio
C. Raphael
D. Giotto
Answer: A

Which Indian artist was known for their contribution to Bengal School of Art?
A. Abanindranath Tagore
B. Raja Ravi Varma
C. Rabindranath Tagore
D. Nandalal Bose
Answer: A

Pablo Picasso's art evolved into how many major periods?
A. 2
B. 3
C. 4
D. 5
Answer: B

Raja Ravi Varma is best known for combining:
A. Indian subjects with European techniques
B. Abstract forms with tribal art
C. Religious themes with surrealism
D. Modern art with Indian folk styles
Answer: A

Part 10: Art Techniques and Mediums
Which tool is commonly used in etching?
A. Burin
B. Palette knife
C. Brush
D. Stylus
Answer: A

What is the term for a sculpture that is carved into a wall?
A. Relief
B. Freestanding
C. Bas-relief
D. High relief
Answer: C

Acrylic paints are primarily made from:
A. Oil
B. Water-based polymer emulsion
C. Wax
D. Egg yolk
Answer: B

Which is NOT a type of brush?
A. Round
B. Flat
C. Spiral
D. Fan
Answer: C

The method of printing using a stone or metal plate is called:
A. Lithography
B. Relief printing
C. Screen printing
D. Digital printing
Answer: A

Tempera is created by mixing pigments with:
A. Oil
B. Water
C. Egg yolk
D. Wax
Answer: C

What is the primary characteristic of a "wash" in watercolor?
A. Thick texture
B. Transparent application
C. Opaque layers
D. Heavy brushstrokes
Answer: B

The term "gesso" is used for:
A. Preparing surfaces for painting
B. Binding pigments in paint
C. Cleaning brushes
D. Thinning paint
Answer: A

Which medium is traditionally used for fresco painting?
A. Oil paint
B. Egg tempera
C. Water-based pigments
D. Acrylic
Answer: C

The technique of "stencil art" is used in which form of printing?
A. Silk screen printing
B. Lithography
C. Etching
D. Relief printing
Answer: A

Part 11: Indian Art and Architecture

The Elephanta Caves are dedicated to which deity?
A. Vishnu
B. Shiva
C. Brahma
D. Durga
Answer: B

What is the primary theme of the Chola bronzes?

A. Royal portraits

B. Buddhist icons

C. Hindu deities

D. Mythological creatures

Answer: C

Which Indian dynasty is associated with the construction of the Khajuraho Temples?

A. Gupta

B. Chola

C. Chandela

D. Maurya

Answer: C

The Mughal emperor Akbar is associated with which style of painting?

A. Pahari

B. Miniature

C. Mysore

D. Warli

Answer: B

The famous Konark Sun Temple was built in the shape of:

A. A mountain

B. A lotus

C. A chariot

D. A palace

Answer: C

Part 12: Design and Visual Arts

Which principle of design emphasizes differences to create interest?

A. Rhythm

B. Contrast

C. Balance

D. Unity

Answer: B

In typography, "serif" refers to:

A. Decorative strokes at the end of letters

B. Bold typeface

C. Text alignment

D. Letter spacing

Answer: A

What is negative space in design?

A. The main subject

B. The area around and between subjects

C. Darker tones

D. Abstract elements

Answer: B

Which color scheme uses three colors equally spaced on the color wheel?

A. Complementary

B. Analogous

C. Triadic

D. Monochromatic

Answer: C

Which type of design focuses on functionality and simplicity?

A. Baroque

B. Modernist

C. Rococo

D. Cubist

Answer: B

Part 13: Art Forms and Media

Which of the following is a traditional art form of Rajasthan?

A. Warli

B. Pattachitra

C. Phad painting

D. Madhubani

Answer: C

Madhubani painting comes from which state in India?

A. Gujarat

B. Bihar

C. Rajasthan

D. Uttar Pradesh

Answer: B

Which of these art forms is closely associated with the Naga tribe of India?

A. Warli painting

B. Pichwai

C. Bamboo crafts

D. Kohima embroidery

Answer: C

Which material is used for the creation of "Tanjore paintings"?

A. Glass

B. Wood and metal

C. Paper

D. Cloth

Answer: B

The technique of using colored sand to create images is called:

A. Sand painting

B. Collage

C. Etching

D. Mosaic

Answer: A

Part 14: Photography and Film

Which aperture setting would allow the most light to reach the film/sensor?

A. f/8

B. f/16

C. f/2.8

D. f/22

Answer: C

In film, the term "mise-en-scène" refers to:

A. The lighting

B. The set design and composition

C. The editing process

D. The soundtrack

Answer: B

The term "bokeh" in photography refers to:

A. The depth of field

B. The quality of the blur in out-of-focus areas

C. The resolution of the image

D. The subject of the photograph

Answer: B

The rule of thirds in photography is used to:

A. Create sharp focus

B. Divide an image into nine equal parts for balanced composition

C. Improve the image resolution

D. Enhance colors

Answer: B

In photography, which setting controls the sensitivity of the film/sensor to light?

A. Shutter speed

B. Aperture

C. ISO

D. Focal length

Answer: C

Part 15: Art Movements and Styles

Which movement is associated with the phrase "art for art's sake"?

A. Realism

B. Impressionism

C. Symbolism

D. Aestheticism

Answer: D

Which of these artists is associated with the Abstract Expressionist movement?

A. Jackson Pollock

B. Claude Monet

C. Leonardo da Vinci

D. Henri Matisse

Answer: A

Which of these terms refers to a painting technique that involves applying paint in thick layers?

A. Glazing

B. Impasto

C. Scumbling

D. Dry brushing

Answer: B

The art style known for its use of geometric shapes and fragmented forms is called:

A. Dadaism

B. Cubism

C. Surrealism

D. Realism

Answer: B

Fauvism is known for the use of:

A. Geometric abstraction

B. Vibrant, non-naturalistic colors

C. Surreal images of dreams

D. Photorealistic techniques

Answer: B

Part 16: Art Materials and Techniques

Which of these is a traditional Indian fabric painting technique?

A. Batik

B. Collage

C. Graffiti

D. Pointillism

Answer: A

What material is used to make watercolor paints?

A. Oil

B. Water

C. Egg yolk

D. Wax

Answer: B

The technique of "cross-hatching" in drawing refers to:

A. Drawing parallel lines in one direction

B. Drawing curved lines to form texture

C. Layering intersecting lines to create tonal value

D. Using dotted patterns to create shading

Answer: C

Which of the following is commonly used to create a smooth finish in oil painting?

A. Glazing

B. Impasto

C. Scumbling

D. Stippling

Answer: A

Which of the following is NOT a primary color in traditional color theory?

A. Red

B. Yellow

C. Green

D. Blue

Answer: C

Part 17: Art History

The artist responsible for the creation of "The School of Athens" fresco is:
A. Raphael
B. Michelangelo
C. Leonardo da Vinci
D. Donatello
Answer: A

Which of the following art movements emerged in the 1950s and 1960s, characterized by its use of mass media imagery?
A. Surrealism
B. Pop Art
C. Dadaism
D. Minimalism
Answer: B

Which of these is a key feature of Baroque art?
A. Use of geometric abstraction
B. Dramatic lighting and intense emotion
C. Use of flat, two-dimensional forms
D. Focus on simplified shapes
Answer: B

The famous painting "The Night Watch" was created by:
A. Rembrandt
B. Vincent van Gogh
C. Gustav Klimt
D. Pablo Picasso
Answer: A

The "Art Nouveau" style is characterized by:
A. Symmetry and order
B. Decorative, flowing patterns inspired by nature
C. Use of geometric forms and abstract patterns
D. Dark and moody themes
Answer: B

Part 18: Sculpture

The famous sculpture "David" was created by which artist?
A. Donatello
B. Leonardo da Vinci
C. Michelangelo
D. Gian Lorenzo Bernini

Answer: C

What type of sculpture involves adding material to form a piece?

A. Carving

B. Casting

C. Modeling

D. Assembling

Answer: C

Which of the following materials is NOT typically used for sculpture?

A. Marble

B. Bronze

C. Glass

D. Canvas

Answer: D

Which sculptor is known for creating "The Thinker"?

A. Henry Moore

B. Auguste Rodin

C. Gian Lorenzo Bernini

D. Alexander Calder

Answer: B

Which of these is an example of a freestanding sculpture?

A. High-relief sculpture

B. Mural

C. Statue of Liberty

D. Bas-relief

Answer: C

Part 19: Visual Arts and Media

What term is used to describe the use of different art forms such as painting, sculpture, and digital media together?

A. Mixed Media

B. Performance Art

C. Installation Art

D. Conceptual Art

Answer: A

Which of these is a method of digital art creation?

A. Watercolor

B. 3D rendering

C. Oil painting

D. Charcoal sketching

Answer: B

In the context of visual arts, "installation art" typically involves:

A. Digital projections

B. Temporary, site-specific arrangements

C. Traditional paintings

D. Interactive sculptures

Answer: B

Which form of art involves performance as part of the creative process?

A. Conceptual art

B. Performance art

C. Mixed media art

D. Surrealism

Answer: B

In digital art, a "pixel" is short for:

A. Pictorial element

B. Picture element

C. Printed element

D. Process element

Answer: B

Part 20: Final Section - Art Criticism and Analysis

Which of the following is a key principle of art criticism?

A. Economic value

B. Formal analysis

C. Popularity

D. The artist's biography

Answer: B

In art, "iconography" refers to:

A. The use of color

B. The use of symbols and imagery

C. The artist's technique

D. The type of material used

Answer: B

The term "formalism" in art criticism refers to focusing on:

A. The narrative content

B. The technique and visual elements of the artwork

C. The artist's intent

D. The socio-political context

Answer: B

Which of the following refers to the emotional impact of a work of art?

A. Formal qualities

B. Expressiveness

C. Content

D. Context

Answer: B

Art criticism involves which of the following steps?

A. Objective description, interpretation, and judgment

B. Only objective description

C. Only personal opinion

D. Just visual analysis

Answer: A

Part 21: Art History and Movements

Which movement is best known for its chaotic and spontaneous style, and is often associated with the works of Jackson Pollock?

A. Surrealism

B. Expressionism

C. Abstract Expressionism

D. Futurism

Answer: C

The "Bauhaus" school of design was founded by:

A. Walter Gropius

B. Frank Lloyd Wright

C. Ludwig Mies van der Rohe

D. Marcel Duchamp

Answer: A

The technique of juxtaposing unexpected elements is a hallmark of which art movement?

A. Cubism

B. Surrealism

C. Dadaism

D. Futurism

Answer: B

Which of these artists is considered a pioneer of the Dada movement?

A. Salvador Dalí

B. André Breton

C. Max Ernst

D. Marcel Duchamp

Answer: D

The term "Impressionism" comes from which famous painting by Claude Monet?

A. Woman with a Parasol

B. Water Lilies

C. Impression, Sunrise

D. Haystacks

Answer: C

Part 22: Color Theory

In color theory, what do complementary colors do?

A. They enhance each other

B. They neutralize each other

C. They create the same color

D. They are always of the same hue

Answer: B

Which color is considered the warmest of primary colors?

A. Blue

B. Red

C. Yellow

D. Green

Answer: B

Which of the following is a secondary color?

A. Red

B. Green

C. Blue

D. Yellow

Answer: B

In the color wheel, which color is opposite green?

A. Blue

B. Red

C. Yellow

D. Orange

Answer: D

In color mixing, what is the result of mixing red and yellow?

A. Orange

B. Green

C. Brown

D. Purple

Answer: A

Part 23: Contemporary Art

Which artist is considered a key figure in the pop art movement?

A. Jackson Pollock

B. Andy Warhol

C. Roy Lichtenstein

D. Claude Monet

Answer: B

Which of the following is a major characteristic of Minimalism?

A. Detailed, realistic depictions

B. Use of simple shapes and limited colors

C. Complex and dramatic compositions

D. Emphasis on symbolism

Answer: B

The term "conceptual art" is associated with which artist?

A. Robert Rauschenberg

B. Yves Klein

C. Sol LeWitt

D. Andy Warhol

Answer: C

Which contemporary artist is known for creating large-scale installations involving light and space?

A. Damien Hirst

B. James Turrell

C. Yayoi Kusama

D. Jeff Koons

Answer: B

The Guggenheim Museum in New York was designed by which architect?

A. Frank Gehry

B. Le Corbusier

C. Frank Lloyd Wright

D. Zaha Hadid

Answer: C

Part 24: Ancient and Classical Art

The Parthenon in Athens was primarily built as a temple dedicated to which deity?

A. Apollo

B. Athena

C. Zeus

D. Hera

Answer: B

The Greek art style characterized by smooth, idealized human forms is known as:

A. Hellenistic

B. Archaic

C. Classical

D. Roman

Answer: C

The "Venus de Milo" sculpture is associated with which civilization?

A. Egyptian

B. Roman

C. Greek

D. Mesopotamian

Answer: C

Which of the following was a famous feature of Roman architecture?

A. Arches

B. Pyramids

C. Ziggurats

D. Obelisks

Answer: A

The famous "Bust of Nefertiti" was discovered in which country?

A. Greece

B. Italy

C. Egypt

D. Iraq

Answer: C

Part 25: Art and Technology

Which digital art program is known for vector-based graphic design?

A. Photoshop

B. Illustrator

C. Procreate

D. CorelDRAW

Answer: B

Which of these tools is commonly used for 3D modeling in digital design?

A. AutoCAD

B. Flash

C. Adobe InDesign

D. Blender

Answer: D

Which of the following is a common file format for web images?

A. TIFF

B. JPEG

C. PSD

D. BMP

Answer: B

In digital design, the term "resolution" refers to:

A. The file size

B. The quality and detail of the image

C. The number of colors in an image

D. The amount of space the design occupies

Answer: B

The use of "layers" in digital design allows for:

A. Multiple edits and adjustments without affecting the whole design

B. A decrease in file size

C. Greater color saturation

D. The image to be flattened into one layer

Answer: A

Part 26: Art Techniques and Styles

Which of the following techniques is associated with the use of dots to create an image?

A. Pointillism

B. Surrealism

C. Impressionism

D. Collage

Answer: A

The technique of "sfumato," used by Leonardo da Vinci, refers to:

A. Glazing

B. Blurring the edges of a painting to create a soft, smoky effect

C. Using bright, contrasting colors

D. Layering thick strokes of paint

Answer: B

Which art technique involves scratching away a surface to reveal the underlying material?

A. Etching

B. Scrimshaw
C. Engraving
D. Sgraffito
Answer: D
Which art style is characterized by distorted, exaggerated forms and is often used to express strong emotions?
A. Surrealism
B. Expressionism
C. Realism
D. Cubism
Answer: B
Which of the following is a feature of "Art Deco" design?
A. Fluid and curvilinear forms
B. Geometric patterns and bold colors
C. Abstract representations
D. Naturalistic forms
Answer: B

Part 27: Art Galleries and Museums
The Louvre Museum is located in which city?
A. New York
B. London
C. Paris
D. Berlin
Answer: C
Which art museum is known for its modern and contemporary art collections in New York City?
A. The Tate Modern
B. The British Museum
C. The Metropolitan Museum of Art
D. The Museum of Modern Art (MoMA)
Answer: D
Which museum is located in Florence and is home to Michelangelo's "David"?
A. The Prado Museum
B. The Uffizi Gallery
C. The Accademia Gallery
D. The Tate Gallery
Answer: C

The British Museum is located in which country?

A. United Kingdom

B. United States

C. Italy

D. France

Answer: A

The National Gallery of Art is located in which city?

A. Washington D.C.

B. Boston

C. San Francisco

D. Chicago

Answer: A

Part 28: Final Section - Miscellaneous

The technique of painting on freshly applied wet plaster is called:

A. Fresco

B. Oil painting

C. Tempera

D. Acrylic painting

Answer: A

Which of the following is the term for a printmaking technique that uses a matrix of metal?

A. Lithography

B. Etching

C. Woodcut

D. Screen printing

Answer: B

The term "Trompe l'oeil" refers to:

A. A painting that fools the eye by mimicking real-life objects

B. A type of abstract art

C. A style of graphic design

D. A monochromatic painting technique

Answer: A

The famous "Wall Street Bull" sculpture is located in which city?

A. Paris

B. New York

C. Chicago

D. London

Answer: B

The French word "Renaissance" means:

A. Revolution

B. Rebirth

C. Beauty

D. Tragedy

Answer: B

Part 29: Art Schools and Institutions

Which of the following is considered one of the most prestigious art schools in India?

A. National Institute of Design (NID)

B. Jawaharlal Nehru University (JNU)

C. Banaras Hindu University (BHU)

D. Delhi University (DU)

Answer: A

The Rhode Island School of Design (RISD) is located in which country?

A. United Kingdom

B. United States

C. France

D. Canada

Answer: B

Which of the following is an art school based in the United Kingdom known for its avant-garde approach to education?

A. The Royal Academy of Arts

B. Goldsmiths, University of London

C. The Slade School of Fine Art

D. Central Saint Martins

Answer: D

The École des Beaux-Arts is located in which city?

A. Berlin

B. Paris

C. New York

D. Florence

Answer: B

Which prestigious Indian art college is located in Mumbai?

A. National Institute of Design (NID)

B. Sir J.J. Institute of Applied Art

C. Banaras Hindu University

D. Government College of Art, Chandigarh

Answer: B

Part 30: Artists and Their Works

Who is known for the iconic sculpture "The Thinker"?

A. Michelangelo

B. Auguste Rodin

C. Pablo Picasso

D. Henri Matisse

Answer: B

Who is the artist behind the famous painting "Guernica"?

A. Pablo Picasso

B. Frida Kahlo

C. Jackson Pollock

D. Andy Warhol

Answer: A

Which artist is known for the "Campbell's Soup Cans" series?

A. Roy Lichtenstein

B. Jackson Pollock

C. Andy Warhol

D. Mark Rothko

Answer: C

The painting "Starry Night" was created by which artist?

A. Henri Matisse

B. Vincent van Gogh

C. Claude Monet

D. Paul Cézanne

Answer: B

Which of the following artists is best known for his large-scale abstract paintings, particularly his "drip paintings"?

A. Jackson Pollock

B. Mark Rothko

C. Frank Stella

D. Salvador Dalí

Answer: A

Part 31: Recent Art Movements and Trends

Which of the following terms is associated with the concept of "creating art from ordinary objects and everyday life"?

A. Pop Art

B. Minimalism

C. Surrealism

D. Conceptual Art

Answer: A

The art movement "Street Art" is closely associated with which of the following?

A. Andy Warhol

B. Banksy

C. Jackson Pollock

D. Pablo Picasso

Answer: B

The "Selfie" culture in art can be traced back to which contemporary art movement?

A. Minimalism

B. Conceptual Art

C. Performance Art

D. Pop Art

Answer: C

The "Instagram Art" phenomenon is characterized by:

A. Hyper-realistic sculptures

B. Art created specifically for social media platforms

C. Traditional techniques in contemporary settings

D. Art inspired by historical periods

Answer: B

Which artist is known for the "Balloon Dog" sculpture, reflecting modern consumerism?

A. Jeff Koons

B. Damien Hirst

C. Banksy

D. Richard Serra

Answer: A

☙

Mock Test Exam

XXV
Mock Test Exam

CUET UG - Fine Arts Domain
  Duration: 45 Minutes
Total Questions: 50
Questions to Attempt: 40
Marking Scheme:
  Correct Answer: +5
  Incorrect Answer: -1
  Unattempted Question: 0
  Instructions:
  Attempt 40 questions only.
  Use the time wisely; each question is important.
  Review your answers before submitting.
  Questions
  Q1. What is the main characteristic of Mughal paintings?
  A) Realistic portraits
  B) Abstract art
  C) Expressionist themes
  D) Surrealism
  Q2. Who painted the famous artwork "Shakuntala"?
  A) Raja Ravi Varma
  B) M.F. Husain
  C) Tyeb Mehta
  D) Nandalal Bose
  Q3. What is the meaning of "Fresco"?
  A) Painting on wet plaster

B) Painting on canvas

C) Etching on a stone surface

D) Sketching with charcoal

Q4. The famous painting "Krishna with Flute" belongs to which school of art?

A) Pahari School

B) Rajasthani School

C) Mughal School

D) Deccani School

Q5. In which medium is the "Ajanta Cave Paintings" created?

A) Oil paint

B) Tempera

C) Watercolor

D) Fresco

Q6. Raja Ravi Varma is known for blending:

A) Indian and European art styles

B) Mughal and Persian styles

C) Abstract and Cubist forms

D) Traditional and Deccani styles

Q7. The use of bright, contrasting colors is a feature of which school of Indian painting?

A) Bengal School

B) Rajasthani School

C) Pahari School

D) Mughal School

Q8. What is "Chiaroscuro" in art?

A) Balance of warm and cool colors

B) Use of light and shadow for dramatic effect

C) Combination of primary colors

D) Fusion of texture and form

Q9. The Deccani School is influenced by which cultural tradition?

A) Chinese

B) Persian

C) Tibetan

D) Mughal

Q10. Which Indian artist is often referred to as the "Father of Modern Indian Art"?

A) Abanindranath Tagore

B) Jamini Roy

C) Nandalal Bose

D) Raja Ravi Varma

Q11. The famous painting "Bharat Mata" was created by:

A) Abanindranath Tagore

B) Rabindranath Tagore

C) Raja Ravi Varma

D) Jamini Roy

Q12. The origin of the Rajasthani School of miniature painting is attributed to which era?

A) 12th Century

B) 16th Century

C) 18th Century

D) 20th Century

Q13. The "Ellora Caves" are most notable for:

A) Frescoes

B) Sculptures

C) Murals

D) Miniature Paintings

Q14. Which Mughal emperor encouraged the growth of miniature paintings?

A) Babur

B) Jahangir

C) Aurangzeb

D) Shah Jahan

Q15. Rabindranath Tagore's art is best described as:

A) Realistic portraiture

B) Abstract and emotive

C) Religious illustrations

D) Depictions of Indian mythology

Q16. Which school of painting focuses primarily on depicting romantic themes such as Radha-Krishna?

A) Rajasthani

B) Pahari

C) Mughal

D) Deccani

Q17. A muralist takes 8 hours to complete a wall. How many walls can they complete in 48 hours?

A) 6

B) 8

C) 10

D) 12

Q18. The Pahari School of painting developed in:

A) Rajasthan

B) Deccan

C) Bengal

D) Himalayan foothills

Q19. Which Indian painting style emphasizes detailed depictions of flora and fauna?

A) Mughal

B) Pahari

C) Bengal

D) Rajasthani

Q20. What is the primary focus of the Bengal School of art?

A) Revival of traditional Indian styles

B) Abstract and conceptual art

C) European academic realism

D) Political caricatures

Q21. Which artist pioneered the use of folk art in modern Indian painting?

A) Jamini Roy

B) Rabindranath Tagore

C) S.H. Raza

D) Tyeb Mehta

Q22. What is the basic principle of perspective in drawing?

A) Using vibrant colors

B) Creating an illusion of depth

C) Highlighting details

D) Simplifying shapes

Q23. The Deccani School is known for:

A) Detailed human anatomy

B) Use of gold and vivid colors

C) Abstract depictions

D) Black-and-white themes

Q24. In art, complementary colors are positioned:

A) Next to each other on the color wheel

B) Directly opposite each other

C) Randomly arranged

D) Triangularly aligned

Q25. The concept of "Wash Technique" is widely associated with:

A) Bengal School

B) Deccani School

C) Mughal Art

D) Pahari Paintings

Q26. "Akbar Nama" is a significant manuscript belonging to which art style?

A) Pahari

B) Mughal

C) Rajasthani

D) Deccani

Q27. What does the term "tempera" refer to in art?

A) Oil-based colors

B) Water-soluble pigments mixed with a binder

C) Fresco technique

D) Sculpture decoration

Q28. Who introduced the "wash technique" in Indian painting?

A) Abanindranath Tagore

B) Jamini Roy

C) Nandalal Bose

D) M.F. Husain

Q29. Which Indian artist was famous for painting traditional Indian women in mythological themes?

A) Raja Ravi Varma

B) Jamini Roy

C) S.H. Raza

D) Tyeb Mehta

Q30. A painting that emphasizes dramatic use of light and dark tones is an example of:

A) Fresco

B) Chiaroscuro

C) Etching

D) Miniature

Q31. Which school of Indian painting is famous for its frescoes?

A) Ajanta

B) Pahari

C) Bengal

D) Mughal

Q32. The Persian miniature tradition heavily influenced which Indian art school?

A) Deccani

B) Rajasthani

C) Mughal

D) Pahari

Q33. What is the purpose of a "grid" in drawing?

A) To add texture

B) To maintain proportions

C) To create abstract effects

D) To highlight shadows

Q34. Nainsukh was an eminent artist of which school of painting?

A) Mughal

B) Pahari

C) Bengal

D) Deccani

Q35. The famous "Elephanta Caves" are associated with which type of art?

A) Miniature

B) Sculpture

C) Fresco

D) Etching

Q36. The term "ground" in painting refers to:

A) The base surface prepared for painting

B) The color of the background

C) The first layer of the painting

D) The texture of the canvas

Q37. The concept of vanishing points is associated with:

A) Color mixing

B) Linear perspective

C) Abstract art

D) Fresco painting

Q38. Which region is known for the Kalamkari style of painting?

A) Rajasthan

B) Andhra Pradesh

C) Himachal Pradesh

D) Kerala

Q39. A color scheme with only black, white, and shades of gray is called:

A) Polychromatic

B) Achromatic

C) Complementary

D) Analogous

Q40. "Gond Art" is primarily practiced in which Indian state?

A) Madhya Pradesh

B) Maharashtra

C) Odisha

D) West Bengal

Q41. What is the significance of warm colors in art?

A) They create a calming effect

B) They evoke energy and warmth

C) They enhance the depth of a painting

D) They soften the composition

Q42. The Kalighat style of painting originated in:

A) Kolkata

B) Bihar

C) Gujarat

D) Assam

Q43. In which painting style is "gold leaf" commonly used?

A) Rajasthani

B) Mughal

C) Deccani

D) All of the above

Q44. Which painting technique uses thin transparent layers of color?

A) Glazing

B) Impasto

C) Scumbling

D) Dry brush

Q45. A triangular composition is often used to:

A) Create balance

B) Highlight colors

C) Emphasize the background

D) Add abstraction

Q46. A painting that primarily uses black and white is an example of:

A) Achromatic composition

B) Analogous colors

C) Saturated palette

D) Monochromatic tones

Q47. What is the primary purpose of "gesture drawing"?

A) To capture motion and energy

B) To create detailed shading

C) To establish color harmony

D) To practice perspective

Q48. Which of the following is a key characteristic of folk art?

A) Uniform style

B) Use of bright and vibrant colors

C) Abstract symbolism

D) Industrial techniques

Q49. Which Indian artist was awarded the Padma Vibhushan for their contributions to modern art?

A) S.H. Raza

B) M.F. Husain

C) Tyeb Mehta

D) Jamini Roy

Q50. What is the term used for carving designs on metal or wood surfaces?

A) Etching

B) Embossing

C) Engraving

D) Chiseling

XXVI
Answer Key

Answer Key for the CUET UG Fine Arts Mock Test

1. A) Realistic portraits
2. A) Raja Ravi Varma
3. A) Painting on wet plaster
4. B) Rajasthani School
5. D) Fresco
6. A) Indian and European art styles
7. B) Rajasthani School
8. B) Use of light and shadow for dramatic effect
9. B) Persian
10. A) Abanindranath Tagore
11. A) Abanindranath Tagore
12. B) 16th Century
13. B) Sculptures
14. B) Jahangir
15. B) Abstract and emotive
16. B) Pahari
17. A) 6
18. D) Himalayan foothills
19. A) Mughal
20. A) Revival of traditional Indian styles
21. A) Jamini Roy
22. B) Creating an illusion of depth
23. B) Use of gold and vivid colors
24. B) Directly opposite each other

25. A) Bengal School
26. B) Mughal
27. B) Water-soluble pigments mixed with a binder
28. A) Abanindranath Tagore
29. A) Raja Ravi Varma
30. B) Chiaroscuro
31. A) Ajanta
32. C) Mughal
33. B) To maintain proportions
34. B) Pahari
35. B) Sculpture
36. A) The base surface prepared for painting
37. B) Linear perspective
38. B) Andhra Pradesh
39. B) Achromatic
40. A) Madhya Pradesh
41. B) They evoke energy and warmth
42. A) Kolkata
43. D) All of the above
44. A) Glazing
45. A) Create balance
46. A) Achromatic composition
47. A) To capture motion and energy
48. B) Use of bright and vibrant colors
49. B) M.F. Husain
50. C) Engraving

ॐ

www.ingramcontent.com/pod-product-compliance
Lightning Source LLC
Chambersburg PA
CBHW040121150726
48005CB00015B/2316